a little NONSENSE
a lot of GOOD SENSE about

IF YOU CHOOSE NOT TO HIT

A Dozen Skills That Make Kids Powerful Problem-Solvers

Written by **KATHY BECKWITH**
Illustrated by **CAROL HENDERSON**

Copyright 2001

Kathy Beckwith and Carol Henderson

ISBN 1-930572-09-3

Library of Congress Catalog Card No. 2001116654

Printing (Last Digit)

       6   5   4   3   2   1

Publisher—

Educational Media Corporation®
P.O. Box 21311
Minneapolis, MN 55421-0311

(763) 781-0088

www.educationalmedia.com

Production editor—

Don L. Sorenson

Graphic design—

Earl Sorenson

Dedication

To Tad and his PeaceBike journey
and with special thanks to
Nancy Carlson, Sharon Michaud, and Gretchen Olson
—Kathy Beckwith

To my daughters, Janelle and Megan, for their
enthusiasm and support; and an added note of thanks to
the many people who posed as models for this book.
—Carol Henderson

About the Author

Kathy Beckwith trains student mediators and works in neighborhood mediation and juvenile victim/offender and parent/teen mediation. She conducts conflict resolution workshops for schools and community groups.

Kathy also enjoys bike riding, walking on the beach, summertime blackberry picking, writing of many kinds, and living and playing with her family, a great source of conflict resolution experiences!

About the Illustrator

Carol Henderson is a freelance artist with a BA in Studio Arts from Pacific University, Oregon. She lives in Tigard, Oregon, with her two daughters and two cats, enjoying many forms of art, writing, music, and dance.

Note to parents, teachers, and other caring adults:

Children's lives can be pretty rough sometimes. They can be bullied, made fun of, left out, belittled, hit, and on some days—all of those things! No child can be his or her best under this kind of attack. Most children learn that they can respond with a similar attack, but this usually just brings on more problems. It doesn't help them understand or stop what was happening in the first place.

Children can learn a better way of problem-solving:

- IF they are encouraged to do it,
- IF they are shown how to do it, and
- IF they see that it really works.

This book shows children some kinds of things they can try if they choose not to hit or use violence. And the "good sense" ideas are mixed in with the "nonsense," just to make it fun.

Parents, I hope you'll forgive me for leaving you stranded back in Dragon Time, but I wanted the kids to know that we as adults are willing to think about what we do, and learn new ways to solve problems too. The book also encourages them to ask you for your ideas of what could be done. You can inspire your children to try, by letting them know you want to help them CHOOSE NOT TO HIT.

My five-year-old and his cousin were arguing over his remote control car. They were loud enough, and our house is small enough, that I knew I was going to have a hard time ignoring this one, even though I had quietly gone to the computer, hoping for some time to write. They found me. A hastily created plan of action worked for 30 seconds or so, and back they came with more woes. I stopped what I was doing, listened, and asked for their ideas. No hint of agreement was in sight. My ten year old daughter had observed the whole incident and asked, "Mom, would you like me to mediate for them?" "YES!" was my instant reply. (She is a member of her school's Mediation Team.) Since she was used to working with a mediator partner at school, she brought in her trolls to help, and sat everyone down in the living room. I couldn't go back to my writing. I hovered just around the corner in the kitchen, amazed at what I heard. In just a few minutes they had their plan, and the tension of the morning had disappeared into play.

We must not underestimate what children can do when they're given the skills! I hadn't thought of a troll/ten-year-old mediation team helping achieve remote control peace! The best part of this book may be the very last question: What can you try?

Kathy

5

Can we buy a copy of this book for Saint George?

I haven't seen him around lately.

To the kids:

When a problem comes up, you have some choices to make:

What am I going to do about this?

How am I going to do it?

For some very good reasons, many kids are choosing not to hit (or fight or name-call or hurt back in other ways). But they're also choosing not to ignore the problem.

How? Read on. You might find a little nonsense, but you also could find a lot of good sense about...

IF YOU CHOOSE NOT TO HIT.

...or can learn

The good sense ideas are skills you may already know.

I'm squished, Mommy. Can I get out and play?

Having a whole pouch full of skills is a good idea. Then you can choose the one that will work best in a particular situation.

They're ready to turn the page, guys. We'd better get in our places.

Hop this way

6

What could you *do* if Jill keeps pulling Maria's braids,
and no one but you is watching?

You might...

Lock her in a castle,
Put a timer on the key
To open up the door again
The day she's 93.

Or you could...

...say, "Jill, Maria, stop! Can I help?"

Skill 1: Stop the Action!

Anger can help. It can show people how important it is to work on a problem. But anger that turns to violence makes a mess. It's much easier to get out of a mess before you get in it, so don't let violence start. Stop the action!

You may be able to Stop the Action for others by calling their names and saying, "Stop. Can I help?" If they say, "Yes," have them tell you, one at a time, what happened. Then help them think of solutions that are good for both of them.

If someone is being mean to you, say, "Stop!" Your voice has power. It shows you are serious and won't let this keep happening. Then choose another skill to solve the problem.

But if anyone is out of control, or if you are afraid, go and get an adult to help.

If it's you who is angry enough to hit, Stop the Action for yourself. Say, "Stop!" out loud, and then do it! If you can't, find someone to help you learn how. Ask other kids how they stop themselves. Ask adults. Keep asking until you find what works for you.

I can see that my friends are going to get themselves into hot water if I don't Stop the Action. "Vise, Nipper—Stop! It's easier to get out of a crab pot before you get in it!"

9

What could you do if you can't stand your brother's teasing anymore, and your fist is saying, "Just hit him hard and he'll stop"?

You might...

Dress him in a bear suit
And take him to the zoo.
Then trade him for an aardvark
Or a friendly kangaroo.

Or you could...

ZOO

...take your fist outside to bounce a ball 37 times. Then think about what happened. When you're feeling calm, come back in and ask your brother if you could talk about teasing.

Skill 2: Cool Down

We often think better and act with better results after we have cooled down.

Sometimes even just a few seconds' pause can make a difference.

Instead of reacting in ways that could make the problem worse, we can remember our choice to be problem-solvers and think about what to do next.

What helps you cool down? Can you take a break from the problem and shoot some hoops, go for a walk or a bike ride, talk to a friend, or take a few slow deep breaths?

I use this skill all the time. A great way to cool down is to spray yourself with your trunk.

But I don't actually have a trunk, so what can I do?

So you can always take some slow, deep rat breaths.

As long as you are alive, you have your breath.

What could you *do* if José comes running up behind you at the park and pushes you out of the swing?

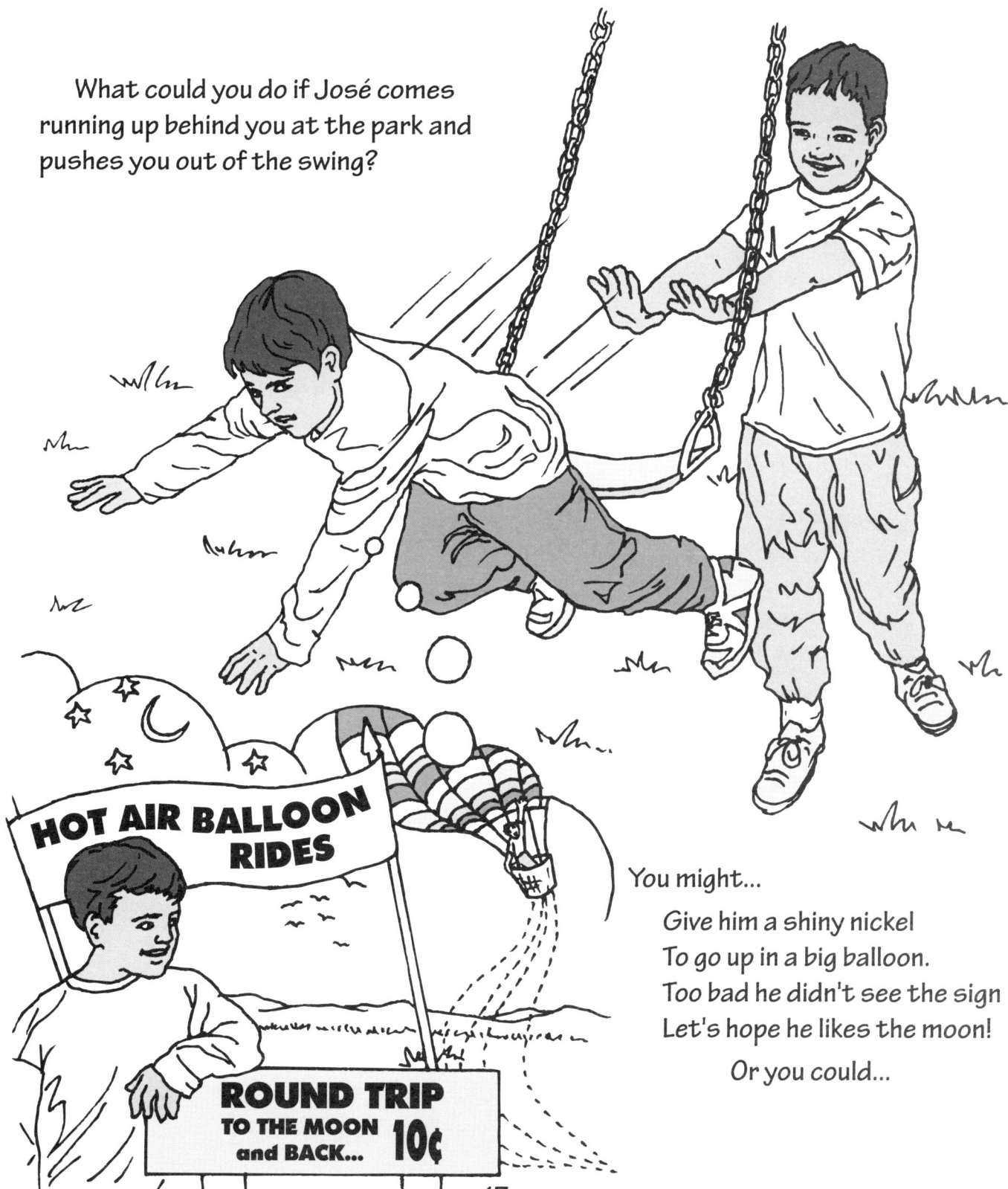

HOT AIR BALLOON RIDES

ROUND TRIP
TO THE MOON
and BACK... 10¢

You might...

Give him a shiny nickel
To go up in a big balloon.
Too bad he didn't see the sign
Let's hope he likes the moon!

Or you could...

...tell José how you feel when you're pushed out of the swing and ask him not to do it anymore. (Is it possible that José thought he was going to be funny giving you a push, and he didn't really think you'd fall out?)

Skill 3: Say How You Feel When...

It takes courage to say how you feel when something hurtful or unkind happens to you. But it's important to do. Then the other person can understand your feelings.

They might apologize or explain something you didn't know before. They might realize that something needs to be different.

But sometimes they'll say, "I don't care!" or "So what?" That's no fun, but try not to be discouraged. You could say, "Maybe we could talk later. This is important to me."

I feel discouraged when I'm called "Slug." I don't like slime trails and I don't wear antennas. I'm a boa constrictor. I'd like to be called Mr. Constrictor.

I didn't know that! Slime trails and antennas are two of my favorite things. I feel proud when I'm called Slug, but I'd be happy to call you Mr. Constrictor.

15

What could you do if someone in your group says she's sick and tired of the way you boss people around, and she's asking the teacher to let her change groups?

CHARACTER

SETTING

You might...

Race her up a mountain
(No rules on how you climb).
You yodel for a mountain goat
And win in record time.

Or you could...

..."bounce back" what she just said, sincerely: "So it seems to you that I'm bossy, and you want to leave our group. Is that right?" Listen carefully to what else she tells you. Then ask if you could explain your viewpoint.

Skill 4: Listen to Learn

When we are criticized or blamed, our first reaction is often to defend ourselves or explain why the other person is wrong. Sometimes we never learn why they said what they did. We end up arguing instead of understanding each other.

It's amazingly hard to do, but if you can get in the habit of "bouncing back" first (putting in your own words what they just said), your criticizer will probably be quite surprised... and will feel more like working with you to solve the problem.

You don't have to agree with them when you bounce back. You're just letting them know you understand their viewpoint. The key is to keep listening and bouncing back and asking questions and listening some more until they feel completely understood.

Then ask if you can explain something they might want to know.

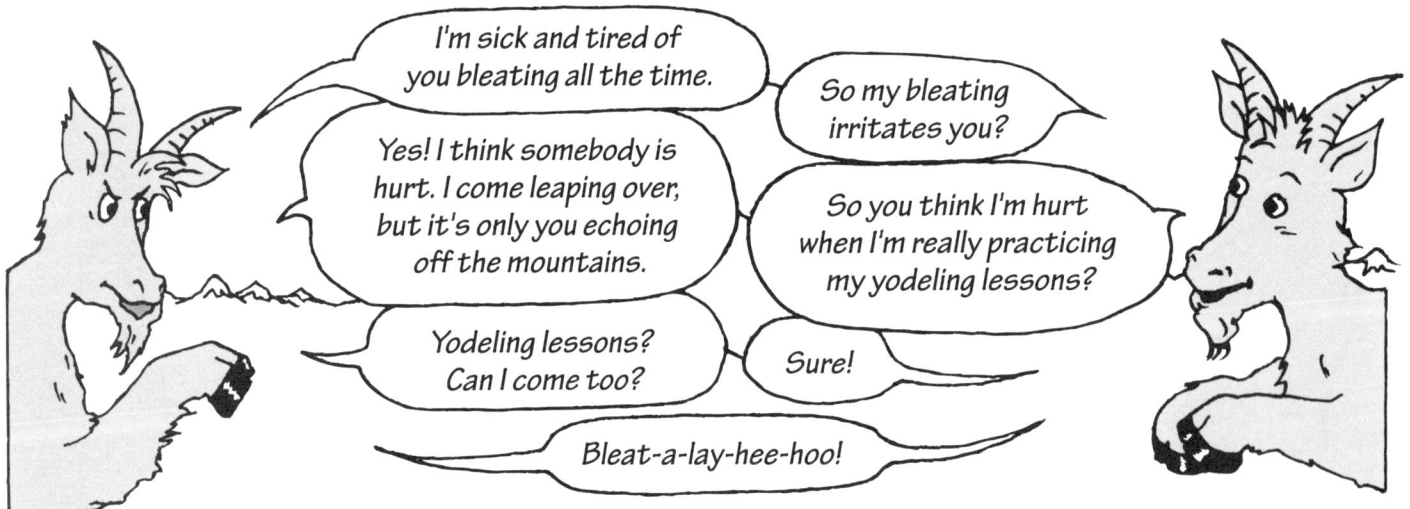

I'm sick and tired of you bleating all the time.

So my bleating irritates you?

Yes! I think somebody is hurt. I come leaping over, but it's only you echoing off the mountains.

So you think I'm hurt when I'm really practicing my yodeling lessons?

Yodeling lessons? Can I come too?

Sure!

Bleat-a-lay-hee-hoo!

What could you do if your mom or dad slaps your feet and yells at you to get your feet off the couch right now?

You might...

Let them try your time machine,
Then play a little joke.
When they arrive in Dragon Time,
Say, "Ooops! The thing just broke."

Or you could...

...put your feet on the floor. Think about the problem and how you were treated. Ask your parents to set aside a time to talk together about what happened.

Skill 5: Think It Over/Talk It Over

Thinking over a problem first makes talking it over easier. What happened? How do you feel? How might the other person feel? What is your part in the problem? What would you like to have happen now?

Talk it over when others aren't listening in. Tell each other what the problem is like for you. "Listen to Learn." Talk one at a time without interrupting. Work for a solution that is respectful and good for both of you.

If someone else asks you to talk about a problem, say to yourself, "This is my lucky day!" even if you don't feel lucky at all. You may learn something that could help both of you.

I'm worried that Mom and Dad won't let me keep the people for pets, after what happened to the last ones. The people might be feeling stressed, or they might love dragons and want to stay here forever. We'll have to talk it over...

Thank you for asking, but we'd rather have a pet than be ones. We think maybe we should be heading home.

21

What could you do if Nick grabs your basketball just as school gets out and runs off with it, and when you ask him for it the next day he says, "Too bad. It's mine now."

You might...

Take him to the dungeon
And let him coach the Rats
On how to steal a basketball
When they play the Bats.

Or you could...

...tell your teacher what happened, and
ask for help to get your basketball back.

Skill 6: Tell and Ask

When a problem is too big for you, tell a helping adult and ask for the help you need. Adults want things to be fair and safe for children, and they will help. If it is an adult who is hurting a child, then you must ask a different adult for help.

Sometimes adults can be so busy or tired that they say, "I don't want to hear about that now." You may need to wait.

Or they might say, "No tattling." Tattling is to get someone in trouble. Telling and asking is different. It is because you need help. You may need to talk to them about that, or just go to someone else this time.

Adults have laws and police and courts to help them when a problem is too big. That is one way they Tell and Ask. You have the right to Tell and Ask too.

My baby is not in my pouch. I let her out to play. She must have been left at the zoo during that switcheroo with the bear. Ellie, can you help me find the way to the zoo?

You bet!

What could you do if a kid in your class comes up and says, "I could smash you if I wanted to!"?

You might...

Put on a super magic show
And ask for volunteers.
First trick: The Kid Becomes a Toad
Last trick: He Disappears!

Or you could...

POOF!

25

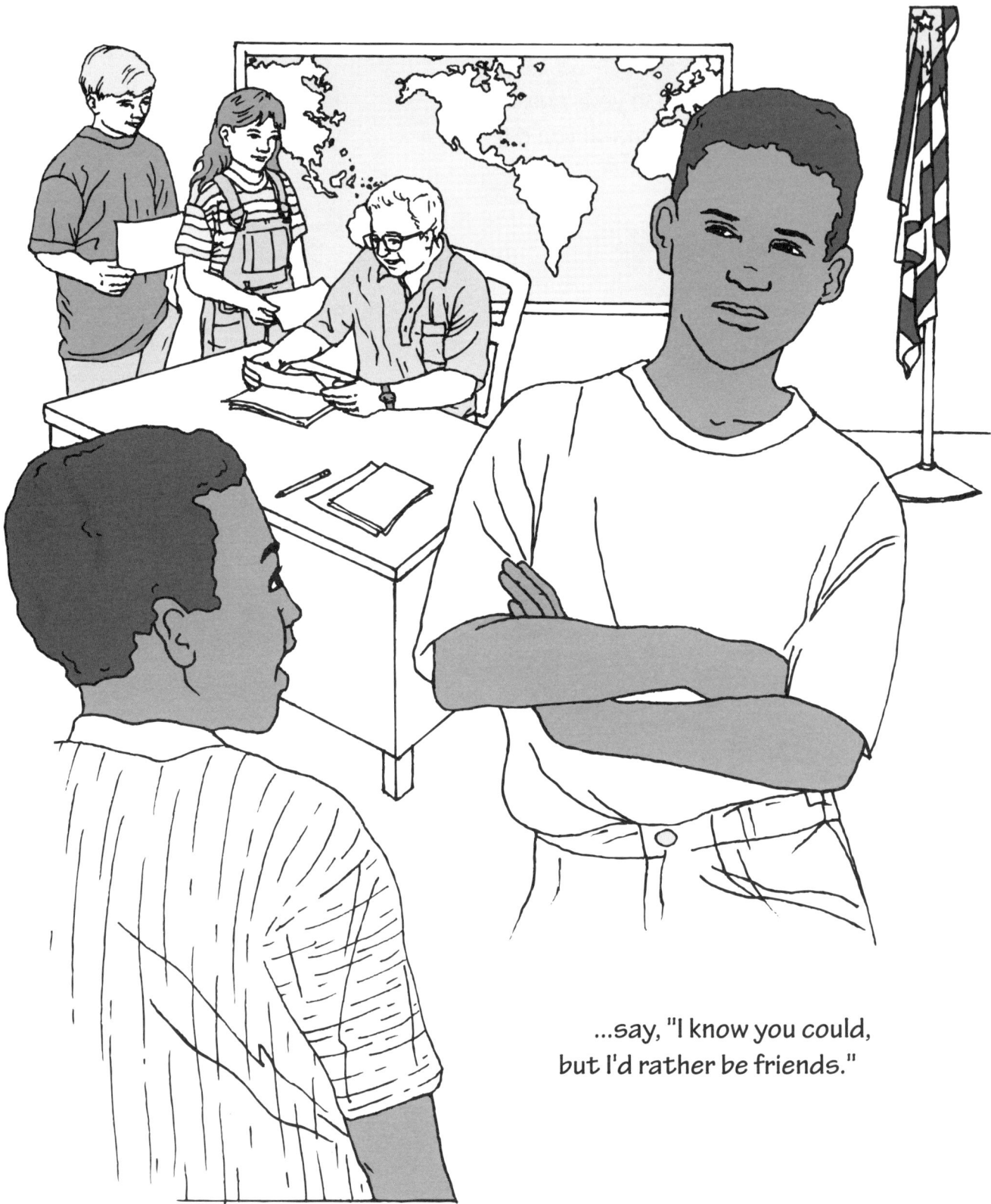

...say, "I know you could, but I'd rather be friends."

Skill 7: Shift Gears

Sometimes kids just bug each other to see what will happen or to make somebody mad. Sometimes the very best thing to do is: Shift Gears!

If they say something ridiculous, answer with something kind. If they want to fight, say "No." If they stick out a leg to trip you when you go to sharpen your pencil, walk on the other side of your desk. If they grab the book you were reaching for, get another book.

But if it's a book you need, or if you're tired of this happening, don't ignore it. Use one of the other skills to solve the problem.

POOF!

Hey, I would have shifted gears, but before I knew what was happening, I was gone.

So now what can I do to get an invisible toad, namely me, Toady, visible again?

What could you *do* if Jo grabs your report on boa constrictors, ripping one of the pictures, and then says, "It serves you right for laughing at my report!"?

You might...

Invite your friends to dinner.
Ask Jo a simple question:
Would sitting next to my pet Slug
Give you indigestion?

Or you could...

...think about why Jo is so mad. Apologize for laughing at her report. When Jo is ready, be willing to accept her apology and let her make amends. (Can she find you another picture, draw one for you, or sharpen your pencils so you can draw another one?)

Skill 8: Apologize and Make Amends

Everybody messes up sometimes. We do things we wish we wouldn't have. Ignoring your mess-ups can leave hurt feelings. It's important to be able to apologize. Holding grudges can keep good things from happening. It's important to be able to accept someone's apology.

Sometimes we'll instantly feel sorry for something we did. Other times we might not even think about it until later, or until someone talks to us about it. When you feel sorry for something you did, it's important to say so.

It's also important to make amends—to do what you can to make up for the damage done or the hurt you caused. It's a fair thing to do. Sometimes you'll know just what to do to make amends. But if it doesn't seem like there's any way to fix the damage, at least talk about what might help.

I'm sorry my yodeling started this little avalanche. Can I help dig you out?

Yodel-ay-ee-oh, magician! I'm over here. Ignoring your mess-up can leave me invisible!

POOF!

What can you do if Meg, who has known your name for two years, keeps calling you "Dog Face" instead?

You might...

Have a peanut eating contest
Between Ellie-phant and Meg.
The loser eats a bale of hay;
The winner eats an egg.

Or you could...

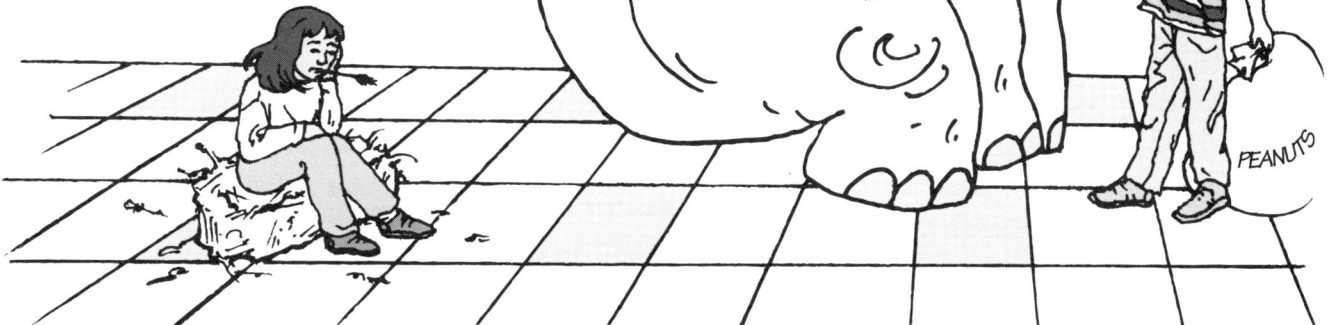

...ask your teacher for a mediation session
so you and Meg could talk about name-calling.

CONFLICT MANAGEMENT WHEEL

WORKSHEET

BRAINSTORMING PAPER

MEDIATION AGREEMENT

SHEET

(If your school doesn't have a mediation team,
maybe this would be a good time to ask about getting
one started.)

Skill 9: Mediate

Many schools are setting up student mediation programs. When two people can't solve a problem, they can ask for mediators to help. Mediators are not judges and don't decide what should be done. They help people understand the problem and each other, and think about solutions that might work.

If your school doesn't have a mediation program, you could ask if they'd do a training, and then volunteer to help. You'll learn great new skills by becoming a mediator, skills you can use for the rest of your life in many different situations. And you'll have fun helping others solve their problems.

She said I have rat breath.

He's always making noises in the dungeon when we're trying to sleep.

Mediation Room
-Welcome-

If I'm still gone when this mediation is over, can you guys mediate for me and that magician kid?

POOF!

What could you do if Sarah invited everyone but you to her party, and you're feeling left out?

You might...
    Buy her a one-way
    Ticket to Rome
    And make her ride
    A turtle back home.

        Or you could...

...plan something else for that day. But if you really care about Sarah's friendship, you could invite her over sometime to look at your pictures of turtles and Rome.

Skill 10: Build Good Relationships

It's fun to do things with people, encourage each other, smile and laugh with each other. Then when a problem comes up, you'll want to solve it so you can get back to doing more fun things.

One of the easiest ways to start a good relationship is to learn a person's name. Then when you see them again, say "Hi," and their name. It makes anyone feel special. Try it!

Even if you don't have much chance to be together or work together on projects, it can make a BIG difference if you have just smiled or been kind to each other when you have met.

Wow, Slug, your shiny slime trails are cool! And the antennas are great for playing space aliens!

Thanks, Mr. C! Do you want to pretend this thing is a spaceship?

Oh, great! My first day back from a long trip, and I have to be a spaceship for some worms!

I'd play too, but it's hard to wear antennas on an invisible head. There must be some way to solve my problem.

POOF!

36

What could you do if Regi pinches you hard every single time you line up for lunch, except on the days he's absent?

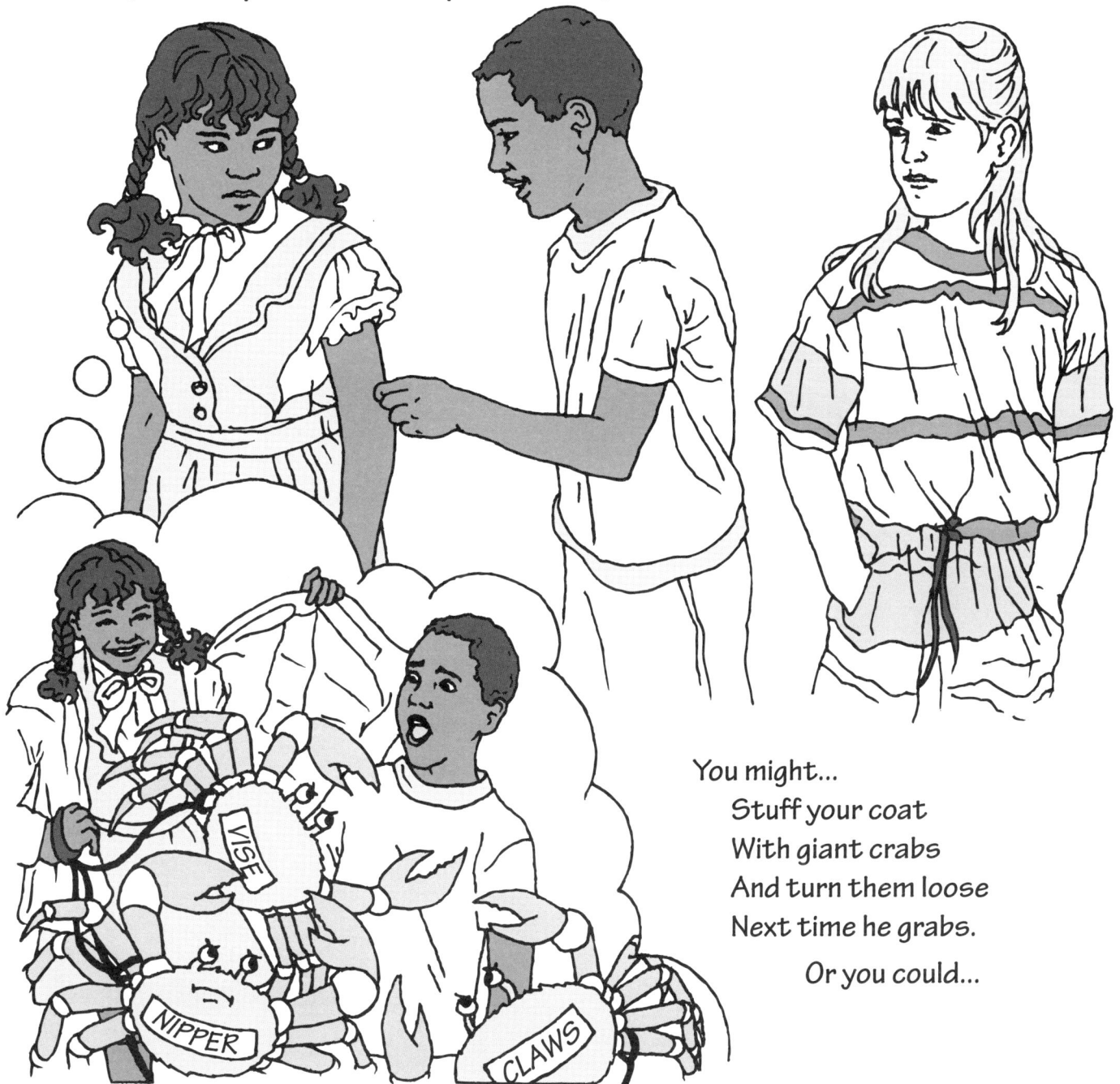

You might...
Stuff your coat
With giant crabs
And turn them loose
Next time he grabs.

Or you could...

...ask your family for an idea of what might work, and try it the next day.

Skill 11: Brainstorm/Make a Plan

There's usually more than one solution to a problem. Get others to brainstorm ideas with you. Try thinking of lots of ideas, even crazy ones. That might help you think of another idea that would work. Don't criticize any ideas yet.

If you're problem-solving with the other person in the conflict, you can brainstorm together. Remember to "Think It Over / Talk It Over" first. Then brainstorm.

Next, evaluate your ideas:

- Would this be good for both of us?
- How could we make it even better?
- Can we really do it?

Keep going until you get a plan you think will work.

Brainstorm List
1. Use time machine for a pet.
2. Dragon can fly people home.
3. Stay for tea and crunchies.

Brainstorm List
1. Find magician.
2. Find magic book.
3. Find me!

POOF!

And what could you do if Regi just laughs and does it again anyway?

That would be hard.

But if you choose not to hit...

40

...there will be another way to solve the problem.

What could you try?

Skill 12: Rely on Your Own Smarts

You may *discover* a new way to solve a problem that is respectful of the other person and really works.

Remember it. Tell others about it. Keep trying. And most important of all, keep choosing not to hit!

I've got it! My own smarts are pulling me through! I know what I can do! Carol... Carol! Can you meet me on the next page? (She's the illustrator of this book.)

POOF!

Yes! I'm going to solve this invisible toad problem once and for all!

Put on a show called:

IF YOU
CHOOSE
NOT
TO HIT

Ahead of time, make signs of the 12 skills
and any other props you want to use.

Stop the Action	Think It Over, Talk It Over	Mediate
Cool Down	Tell and Ask	Build Good Relationships
Say How You Feel When...	Shift Gears	Brainstorm, Make a Plan
Listen to Learn	Apologize and Make Amends	Rely On Your Own Smarts

At show time:

Read:

Reader #1 reads

"What could you do if...."

Reader #2 (dressed in a silly costume) reads the nonsense

"You might...."

Reader #3 reads the good sense

"You could...."

Act:

Divide the signs among you. Using the information about the skills, put on short role plays to show each skill being used to solve a problem.

Then...

Take a bow!

The End

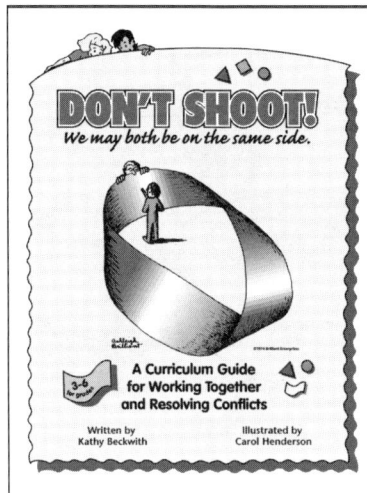